SABZKHAN

Idioms & Sayings

محاورے اور کہاوتیں

Mohawrey & Kahavatein

A compilation of the finest, most interesting and deep rooted ethics enriched Idioms and Sayings.

SABZKHAN

FastPrint Publishing
www.fast-print.net/store.php

IDIOMS & SAYINGS

محاورے اور کہاوتیں

MOHAWREY & KAHAVATEIN

A catalogue record for this book is available from the British Library

ISBN 978-178456-231-1

First published 2015 by
FASTPRINT PUBLISHING
Peterborough, England.

DEDICATION

Bismillah Ir Rahman Nir Rahim

بِسْمِ اللهِ الرَّحْمٰنِ الرَّحِيْمِ

"In the name of God,

Most Gracious,

Most Compassionate"

PREFACE

Message from the Author

Hi there readers,

I, Sabeena Khan being a British born Pakistani and an educationalist have embarked upon the mission to produce learning resource aids for British Pakistanis firstly to promote Urdu.

I have dedicated my work towards the development of the Urdu language for British Asians in the UK. In light of the loss of language that is currently being felt amongst users of the Urdu language, these efforts are to bring to the surface and aid many aspects of the Urdu language through the use of the Roman format as an aid to assist the learner in getting to the original Urdu script.

Whilst each language has its own flavour in the manner in which the language is constructed and used, many similarities are evident. This book aims to identify similar ***Idioms*** and ***Sayings*** that are expressed and used both in the English language and in the Urdu language. The Urdu being ***Mohawrey*** and ***Kahavatein***.

Being brought up in the West, the reality is that our strengths lie in English, which suggests that we may possibly be more familiar with the English ***Idioms*** and ***Sayings*** nevertheless the comparison of ***Mohawrey*** and ***Kahavatein*** comes as a surprising eye opener and gives way for some fun discussion and acts as a resource aid in the learning of Urdu.

SABZKHAN

A selected few Idioms and Sayings are the seeds I planted to introduce to you an interesting read and to start you off in way of searching to develop your skills and knowledge further.

'Khud he liko ge tum apne kismet ke kahani Sabz,

Keh teh hai bas tumara ana or tumhara jana...'

Thank you

Sabeena Khan

UK Published Author

KADAM/STEPS

RAHEIN/ THE WAY

Pewasta rahe shajaar se umeed-e-bahaar rak.

پیوستہ رہے شجر سے

اُمیدِ بہار رکھ

Allama Iqbal (1877-1938)

Agerch-e-bhut hain
jamaat ke aasteeno me,

mujy hai hukmain aazan

La Illah ha Illala

اگرچہ بت ہیں جماعت کی آستینوں میں

مجھے ہے حکمِ اذاں

لَا اِلٰہ اِلَّا اللّٰہ

Allama Iqbal (1877-1938)

Leb javeh teh vand deyda,

na labeh teh shukkar

kar leyda.

لبھ جاوے تے ونڈ دیئدا،

نا لبھے تے شُکر

کرلئی دا۔

Maullana Romi (1207-1278)

CONTENTS

ENGLISH TEXT

ROMAN URDU TEXT

URDU TEXT

IDIOMS / MOHAWREY

When expressing yourself in Urdu, you may be pleasantly surprised to learn that Urdu also shares Idioms that mean that same as they would in the English language.

So, what are Idioms?

Idioms are groups of words that have a meaning that is often impossible to work out alone as the words are not meant what they are directly translated to mean.

This is because they are said in reference to an idea or belief that has no present value. It's an expression of feelings and ideas using everyday words in a special manner to mean something other than what they translate to mean.

Ups and downs

Nashaibo Faraz

نشیب و

Once in a blue moon

Eid ka chand hona

عید کا چاند ہونا

Under the weather

Tabeeyat kharab

طبیعت خراب

The spitting image

Hoo baa hoo

ہو بہو

Nor turn a hair

Baal beinga hona

بال بینگا ہونا

Out of the blue

Demaag se bahar

دماغ سے باہ

Back to square one

Phir alif se shuroo hona

پھر الف سے شروع ہونا

Breaking the ice

Khamoshi torna

خاموشی توڑنا

Jack of all trades

Khud mukhtiar

خودمختیار

White lie

Safaid jhoot

سفید جھوٹ

By hook or by crook

Jaiz or najaiz tareeke se

جائز اور ناجائز طریقے سے

With open arms

Josh o kharosh
se

جوش وخروش سے

In broad daylight

Din dehari

دن دیہاڑے

A honey tongue, a heart of gall

Bagal me chori, moun me raam raam

بغل میں چھری منہ میں رام رام

A little knowledge is a dangerous thing

Neem hakeem khatra-e- jaan

نیم حکیم خطرہِ جان

Haste makes waste

Ageh dor, pecheh chor

آگے دوڑ پیچھے چھوڑ

A friend in need is a friend indeed

Dost wohi joh museebat meh kaam aye

ست وہی جو مصیبت میں کام آئے

Empty vessel makes much noise

(1)Oucha bartan chalakta hai

اُچھا برتن چھلکتا ہے

(2)Thotha chana, baje ghana

تھوتھا چنا باجے گھنا

One beats the bush, another takes the birds

(1)Kamae dhoti wala, khaiy topi wala

کمائے دھوتی والا کھائے ٹوپی والا

(2)Ande seeve koi, bache leve koi

انڈے سیوے کوئی بچے لیوے کوئی

Let the cat out of the bag

Zara pata toh lage

ذرا پتا تو چلے

Hit the nail on the head

Teer nishane pe aya

تیر نشان پے آیا

Show somebody the ropes

Kissi ko rasta dikana

کسی کو راستہ دکھانا

SABZKHAN

SAYINGS/ KAHAVATEIN

When expressing yourself in Urdu, you may be pleasantly surprised to learn that Urdu also shares some sayings that are also expressed in the English language but the same meaning is being expressed.

So, what are Sayings?

Sayings are short, pithy, commonly known and used expression that are used to deliver a message of advice and wisdom.

Much wisdom is derived from trying to understand the message of wisdom behind the saying. It can be open to different interpretations and reflects some moral, story or history.

A bad beginning
makes a bad end.

Agaaz bura,
Anjaam bura.

آغاز بُرا انجام بُرا

A wish coming true.

Andha kya chahe do ankeh.

اندھا چاہے دو آنکھیں

The grass is always greener on the other side.

Door ke dhol suhane.

دور کے ڈھول سُہانے

A person of no principal.

Ganga gayi ganga des, jamna gayi jamna des.

گنگا گئی گنگا دیس جمنا گئی جمنا دیس

Division is the main reason for the damage.

Ghar ka bhedi lanka dhaye.

گھر کا بھیدی لنکا ڈھائے

To the good the world appears good.

Aap bhala toh jag bhala.

آپ بھلا جگ بھلا

Truth is bitter.

Saachi baat karvi
hoti hai.

سچی بات کڑوی ہوتی ہے

Hard work always pays.

Mehnat he sab se bari dolat hain.

محنت ہی سب سے بڑی دولت ہے

Health is wealth.

(1)Tanddrusti hazar nehmat hain.

تندرُستی ہزار نعمت ہے

(2)Jaan hai toh jahaan hai.

جان ہے تو جہان ہے

Truth always
wins.

Hamesha saach
ke jeet hoti hain.

ہمیشہ سچ کی جیت ہوتی ہے

All are not alike.

Pancho ungliyaan barabar nahi hoti.

پانچوں اُنگلیاں برابر نہیں ہوتی

Courtesy costs nothing.

Sharafaat me kuch kharch nahi hota.

شرفت میں کچھ خرچ نہیں ہوتا

Perseverance prevails.

Istakamat meh hasool-e-maqsad hai.

اِستقامت میں حصولِ مقصد ہے

Man is slave to his stomach.

Admi pait ka gulam hai.

آدمی پیٹ کا غلام ہے

Those that save,
leave it all
behind.

Joh jor gaya, woh
chor gaya.

جو جوڑ گیا وہ چھوڑ گیا

Death pays all debts.

Mar gaye, mukar gaye.

مر گئے مکر گئے

A bad coin always returns.

Khota sika hamesha lot atta hai.

کھوٹا سکہ ہمیشہ لوٹ آتا ہے

Every ass loves his bray.

(1)Har ghade ko apni awaaz hi soreeli lagti hai.

ہر گدھے کو اپنی آواز ہی سُریلی لگتی ہے

(2)Har bewakoof khud ko samajdaar samajta hai.

ہر بیوقوف خود کو سمجھدار سمجھتا ہے

Give a dog a bad name and hang him.

Kissi ho marna ho to ilzaam de kar maro.

کسی کو مارنا ہو تو الزام دے کر مارو

Handsome is that handsome does.

Khoobsoorat woh joh khoobsoorat kaam kare.

خوبصورت وہ جو خوبصورت کام کرے

Sour grapes.

Haat na pohnche,
thu khatta.

ہاتھ نہ پُہنچے تھو کھٹا

Your own drown you.

Ghar ka bhedi lanka dhaye.

گھر کا بھیدی لنکا ڈھائے

SPECIAL FEATURE

ZUBAAN KI KADAR AYE GI...

زبان کی قدر آئے گی

NOW YOU WILL LEARN THE VALUES OF LANGUAGE...

(Extracted from Rahein, The Way, Sabz Khan 2015.)

Learning breeds controversy.

Ilm me ikhtalaaf hona fitri hai.

علم میں اختلاف ہونا فطری ہے

Praising at your face is flattery.

Moo pe ki gaye tareef khushamad hoti hai.

منہ پے کی گئی تعریف خوشامد ہوتی ہے

Nothing is permanent in this world.

Duniya me sabaat nahi.

دُنیا میں ثبات نہیں

(1)Experience will teach the unskilled.

----

(2)Practice makes perfect.

Kaam ko kaam sikhata hai.

کام کو کام سِکھاتا ہے

Familiarity breeds contempt.

Kadar kam kar deta hai har roz ka ana jana.

قدر کم کر دیتا ہے ہر روز کا آنا جانا

Birds of the same fleet flock together.

Aik theli ke chatte batte.

ایک تھیلی کے چٹے بٹے

Many heads,
many minds.

Apne apne dafli,
apna apna raag.

اپنی اپنی ڈفلی اپنا اپنا راگ

Society moulds man.

Kharbooza kharbooze ko dehk ke rang pakarta hai.

خربوزہ خربوزے کو دیکھ کے رنگ پکڑتا ہے

A thing is valued where it belongs.

(1)Jungle me moti ki kadar nahi hoti.

جنگل میں موتی کی قدر نہیں ہوتی

(2)Johri jany heere ki kadar.

جوہری جانے ہیرے کی قدر

A stitch in time saves nine.

Waqt ka ek tanka bewaqt ke no tanko se behtar hai.

وقت کا ایک ٹانکا بے وقت کے نو ٹانکوں سے بہتر ہے

Save what you can.

Baaghte chor ki langoti hi sahi.

بھاگتے چور کی لنگوٹی ہی سہی

Something for nothing.

Muft meh jo haath aye to bura kya.

مُفت میں جو ہاتھ آئے بُرا کیا ہے

A stitch in time saves nine.

Gaya waqat phir haath nahi atta.

گیا وقت پھر ہاتھ آتا نہیں

Nobody does something for nothing.

Harkat meh barkat hai.

حرکت میں برکت ہے

ACTIVITIES

Activity 1

1. **Read** the idiom from the text
2. **Write** the idiom
3. **Discuss** the idiom
4. **Explain** the idiom
5. **Illustrate** the idiom
6. Place the idiom in a scenario situation using **role play**, apply the correct tone to emphasis its meaning accurately.

(Task: written, verbal, discussion, role play, visual)

Recording Sheet

Read from page ____

Illustration →

Idiom:

Discussion notes:

The idiom means:

Activity 2

1. **Think** of the idioms that you use, may have heard of or come across.
2. **List** the idioms
3. What was the context of the situation? **Analyse** and **Discuss**
4. **Explain** the idiom
5. **Illustrate** the idiom
6. Place the idiom in a scenario situation using **role play**, apply the correct tone to emphasis its meaning accurately.

(Task: written, verbal, discussion, role play, visual)

Recording Sheet

Illustration →

Idiom:

Discussion notes:

The idiom means:

Activity 3

1. **Read** the saying from the text
2. **Write** the saying
3. **Discuss** the saying
4. **Explain** the saying
5. **Illustrate** the saying
6. Place the saying in a scenario situation using **role play**, apply the correct intonation to emphasis its meaning accurately.

(Task: written, verbal, discussion, role play, visual)

Recording Sheet

Read from page ____

Illustration →

Saying:

Discussion notes:

The saying means:

Activity 4

1. **Think** of the sayings that you use, you may have heard of, or come across.
2. **List** the saying
3. What was the context of the situation? **Analyse** and **Discuss**
4. **Explain** the saying
5. **Illustrate** the saying
6. Place the saying in a scenario situation using **role play**, apply the correct tone to emphasis its meaning accurately.

(Task: written, verbal, discussion, role play, visual)

NOW YOU WILL LEARN THE VALUES OF LANGUAGE...

Now you will learn the values of

language...

When you become engrossed in the lifestyle and culture of the West,

Then you will remember your motherland,

And so you will return, but the children will be in great difficulty.

ZUBAAN KI KADAR AYE GI...

زبان کی قدر آئے گی

Zubaan ki kadar aye gi...

زبان کی قدر آئے گی

Jab jakrey jao ge magrib ki
zanjeeron me,

جب جکڑے جاؤ گے مغرب کی زنجیروں میں

Phir apne wattan ki yaadaye gi,

پھر اپنے وطن کی یاد آئے گی

To lot ke woh wapas ayen ge or
nasal mushkil me par jaye gi,

تو لوٹ کے وہ واپس آئیں گے اور نسل مُشکل میں پڑ جائے گی

The link would have been weakened.

The blind fold of money would have taken its toll.

Now even the thought of poverty would make you all cringe.

No longer is there any patience left.

The off-spring will run back to their Western homes.

Keh woh jor kamzor ho chuka
hoga,
کہ وہ جوڑ کمزور ہو چکا ہوگا

Peson ki patti char gayei hoge,
پیسوں کی پٹی چڑ گئی ہو گی

Gurbat se nafrat ab to aye gi,
غربت سے نفرت اب تو آئے گی

Koi saber naa ho paye ga,
کوئی صبر نہ ہو پائے گا

Bache wappis magrib ke ghar tak
bhagen ge,

بچے واپس مغرب کے گھر تک بھاگے گے

Parents will seek forgiveness from
their elders and families,

And some will shed tears of blood.

This realisation will now trigger
them to think...

How can this gap be erased?

How can their love be enhanced?

Valedain baro se maafi mange ge,
والدین بڑوں سے معافی مانگے گے

Orr kuch khoon ke ansoo royen ge,
اور کچھ خون کے آنسو روئے گے

Majboor ho ke sochen ge...
مجبور ہو کے سوچیں گے

Keh is fasle ko door hum kese kare?
کہ اس فاصلے کو دور ہم کیسے کریں

Pyar, mohobat kese barhaein?
پیار محبت کیسے بڑھائیں

How can we mould our children
towards being more respectful and
obedient?

How can we instil our Eastern
culture and values?

So, now you have begun to value
the worth of your language,

And what you have lost.

Now you will re-educate the
children and generations to come,

Bache farmabardar kese karein?

بچے فرمانبردار کیسے کریں

Mashriki mahol kese banaein?

مشرقی ماحول کیسے بنائیں

Phir zubaan ki kadar aye gi,

پھر زبان کی قدر آئے گی

Keh kya humne koya hai,

کہ کیا ہم نے کھویا ہے

Phir agli nasal ko hum samjayein ge,

پھر اگلی نسل کو ہم سمجھائیں گے

Transferring your language skills,
the etiquettes & mannerism that it
teaches,

It will now take form as your
weapon.

For this generation will make us
meet,

They will take us to the East,

Ancestors will now rest peacefully,

For a new seed of hope has been
planted,

Zubaan ki taleem or adab hum sikayein ge,

زبان کی تعلیم اور ادب ہم سِکھائیں گے

Ise apna hathyaar banayein ge,

اِسے اپنا ہتھیار بنائیں گے

Keh woh nasal phir humain milaye gi,

کہ وہ نسل پھر ہمیں مِلائے گی

Or mashrik le jaye gi,

اور مشرِق لے جائے گی

Tabhi purkhon ko saqoon aye ga,

تبھی پُرکھوں کو سکون آئے گا

Or naye sire se aik umeed jaage gi,

اور نئے سِرے سے ایک اُمید جاگے گی

Our Eastern language will have delivered its flavour,

Now you have begun to value your language...

Mashriqi zubaan apna asar chor
jaye gi,

مشرقی زبان اپنا اثر چھوڑ جائے گی

Ab zubaan ki kadaar aye gi...
اب زبان کی قدر آئے گی

ND - #0193 - 060826 - C2 - 216/138/8 - PB - 9781784562311 - Gloss Lamination